FOOD WEBS

T0014378

FOREST

Food Webs

By William Anthony

KidHaven
PUBLISHING

Published in 2021 by
KidHaven Publishing, an Imprint of Greenhaven Publishing, LLC
353 3rd Avenue
Suite 255
New York, NY 10010

© 2021 Booklife Publishing
This edition is published by arrangement with Booklife Publishing

All rights reserved. No part of this book may be reproduced in any form
without permission in writing from the publisher, except by a reviewer.

Edited by: Madeline Tyler
Designed by: Jasmine Pointer

Find us on

Cataloging-in-Publication Data

Names: Anthony, William.
Title: Forest food webs / William Anthony.
Description: New York : KidHaven Publishing, 2021. | Series: Food webs |
Includes glossary and index.
Identifiers: ISBN 9781534535169 (pbk.) | ISBN 9781534535183 (library bound) |
ISBN 9781534535176 (6 pack) | ISBN 9781534535190 (ebook)
Subjects: LCSH: Forest ecology--Juvenile literature. | Forest plants--Juvenile
literature. | Forest animals--Juvenile literature. | Food chains (Ecology)--Juvenile
literature.
Classification: LCC QH541.5.F6 A584 2021 | DDC 577.3--dc23

Printed in the United States of America

CPSIA compliance information: Batch #BS20K: For further information contact Greenhaven
Publishing LLC, New York, New York at 1-844-317-7404.

Please visit our website, www.greenhavenpublishing.com. For a free color
catalog of all our high-quality books, call toll free 1-844-317-7404 or fax
1-844-317-7405.

Photo credits:
Images are courtesy of Shutterstock.com with thanks to Getty Images, Thinkstock Photo, and iStockphoto.

aradaphotography (soil), YamabikaY (paper texture). Front cover - Erik Mandre, Eurospiders, Eric Isselee, Mariyana M, EKramar, Lillac.
2 - Marcin Perkowski. 3 - Mariyana M. 4 - Artem Kniaz. 6 - Ihor Bondarenko, NTaenk. 6 - 99Art, Anna Luopa, Aenyeth. 7 - Marcin Pencowski, Josef
Pittner, miroslav chytil. 6 & 7 - Ake13bk. 8 - Erik Mandre. 9 - Svietlieisha Olena, Jeff McGraw, Richard Seeley, FotograFFF. 10 - Michael Liggett, Aleksey
Stemmer. 11 - Valentyna Chukhlyebova, Anna Luopa, Tom Meaker. 12 - William Eugene Dummitt. 13 - Richard Seeley, Frank Fichtmueller, Tom Tietz,
Chase Dekker. 14 - BMJ. 15 - Scott E Read, Josef Pittner, miroslav chytil, Jody Ann. 16 - Geoffrey Kuchera. 17 - Eric Isselee, Marcin Perkowski, Aenyeth.
18 - Luke23. 19 - photomaster, Don Mammoser. 20 - critterbiz. 21 - Martin Mecnarowski.

CONTENTS

Words that look like THIS can be found in the glossary on page 24.

IN THE FOREST

Go for a walk, explore between the trees... but be careful!
Do you know who might be hiding in the woods, looking
for a snack?

There are lots of different animals and plants to be found, all going about their daily business, and each and every one of them has a place in the food web.

Let's look at who eats who in the forest.
This is an Alaskan forest in North America.
Let's see what we can find...

...eat the plants...

It all starts with the sun's energy...

...which feeds plants...

eat the herbivores...

...bigger PREDATORS eat them...

...and APEX PREDATORS eat those.

THE GRIZZLY BEAR

Careful—I may look cuddly, but don't come too close. I'm a grizzly bear, and I'm an apex predator, which means nothing tries to eat me. I'm no ordinary bear— I'm one of the deadliest bears on the planet, and I'm hungry...

NAME:	North American Brown Bear
TYPE:	MAMMAL
HOME:	North America
FOOD:	OMNIVORE
PREDATOR OR PREY?	Apex Predator

There are so many options on the menu for me.

Berries: small but sweet...?

Dall sheep: feisty but fantastic...?

Caribou: they have weapons but they're wonderful...?

No, I want something bigger. I think a moose would fill me up!

THE RACE IS ON!

THE MOOSE

Phew, I need to catch my breath! That bear and I run at almost the same speed, so I was lucky to get away! I'm a moose, and while I may look big and scary, I just enjoy a nice leaf-based lunch!

NAME:	Moose
TYPE:	Mammal
HOME:	North America, Northern Europe, and Northern Asia
FOOD:	Herbivore
PREDATOR OR PREY?	Prey

Tree leaves: leafy and lovely...?

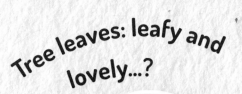

Shrubs: green and great...?

Flowers: pretty and tasty...?

I'm so tired after that lucky escape that I just want an easy meal—I'm going for the tree leaves! I'll leave the other two for other animals.

WHO ELSE EATS PLANTS?

THE DALL SHEEP

I'm a Dall sheep, and I'm an herbivore too, just like that big moose. That means I eat the same food as him. I'm so glad he went for the tree leaves; I've got enough animals to compete with for food!

NAME:	Dall Sheep
TYPE:	Mammal
HOME:	North America
FOOD:	Herbivore
PREDATOR OR PREY?	Prey

All of these animals are trying to eat the same food as me!

Moose: magnificent but massive...

Beaver: they're cute, but they bite...

Caribou: awesome, but they have antlers...

They're all so difficult to get rid of! Wait, is that a bobcat? I think she's spotted the beaver, but she hasn't spotted me. Yay!

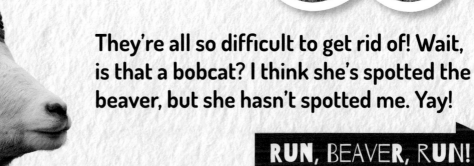

RUN, BEAVER, RUN!

THE BEAVER

Can this day get any worse? I'm a beaver, and I have quite a few predators that I need to keep a lookout for. Still, I didn't expect to have all of them chasing after me in one day; I just want to eat in peace!

NAME:	Beaver
TYPE:	Mammal
HOME:	North America, Europe, and Asia
FOOD:	Herbivore
PREDATOR OR PREY?	Prey

I've had to hide from all these predators just today!

Coyote: sneaky and scary...

Grizzly bear: huge and horrifying...

Wolf: fearsome and fast...

Lucky for me, I can hide in my <u>DAM</u> when something is coming! Excuse me— I think I see a bobcat. Bye!

OFF I GO!

15

THE BOBCAT

That sneaky beaver! Next time, he's going to be my appetizer, main course, and dessert all at once! For now, though, there are other options here on land—I'm not really a swimmer. I'm a carnivore, which means that lots of animals are on my dinner menu.

NAME:	Bobcat
TYPE:	Mammal
HOME:	North America
FOOD:	Carnivore
PREDATOR OR PREY?	Both

Red fox: a sly reward...?

Dall sheep: a furry feast...?

Rabbit: a speedy supper...?

They're all excellent meals, but in the end there's only one winner. Rabbits are my favorite food. Let's hope I can eat my meal before the apex predator shows up.

WHO'S THE APEX?

THE WOLF

I'm a wolf, and just like the grizzly bear, I'm an apex predator. What puts me at the top of the food web isn't just my own skill, it's the skills of my PACK. We hunt for our dinner together because using teamwork is better than hunting alone.

NAME:	Wolf
TYPE:	Mammal
HOME:	North America, Europe, and Asia
FOOD:	Carnivore
PREDATOR OR PREY?	Apex Predator

Depending on what we want for dinner, the pack will need to change how we hunt.

Beaver: a small snack but very tasty...?

Bobcat: hard to find but delicious...?

Moose: strong but a big meal...?

It's the moose for us today. There are many mouths to feed in the pack, so we need a bigger dinner! There's one big animal we won't try to eat, though.

FIND OUT WHO! ➤

19

APEX VS. APEX

We don't try to eat the forest's other apex predator, the grizzly bear. We eat a lot of the same food as the fully grown grizzly bear, but he's not worth the fight. He's much stronger than we are and could hurt us badly.

I won't try to eat the wolves. It's not a good idea for me because I am on my own and they are in a group. They could outnumber me, and then I'd be in trouble. We're hardly ever on each other's menus!

Bears and wolves very rarely fight because their weaknesses are the other's strengths.

FOREST FOOD WEB

The arrows follow where the energy goes. Can you follow the energy from the sun all the way to the grizzly bear and wolf?

RED FOX

BOBCAT

WOLF

DALL SHEEP

COYOTE

GRIZZLY BEAR

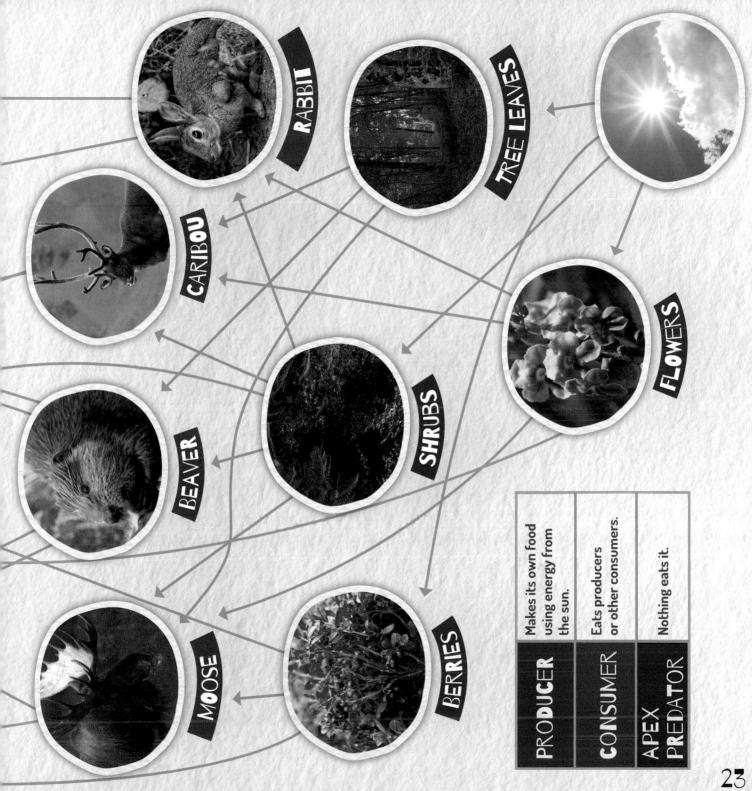

RABBIT

TREE LEAVES

CARIBOU

FLOWERS

BEAVER

SHRUBS

MOOSE

BERRIES

PRODUCER	CONSUMER	APEX PREDATOR
Makes its own food using energy from the sun.	Eats producers or other consumers.	Nothing eats it.

GLOSSARY

apex predator	The top predator in a food chain, with no natural predators of its own.
carnivore	An animal that eats other animals instead of plants.
dam	A barrier made of branches and sticks that holds back the water and provides a home for beavers.
herbivore	An animal that eats plants instead of other animals.
mammal	An animal that has warm blood, a backbone, and produces milk.
omnivore	An animal that eats both plants and other animals.
pack	A group of the same animal (for example, wolves).
predator	An animal that hunts other animals for food.
prey	Animals that are hunted for food.

INDEX